FEMALE DUMB DOWN

COMMIE NUTHOUSE

Illustrations and Theory
by Karen Kellock Ph.D.

This is a new theory in psychology. According to Koestler, all landmark theories are presented in picture-strip format (right-left integration) to bring on the "aha" experience of the formula (the characteristic of all new paradigms).

FORMULA FOR THEORY:

ALL SUCCESS ATTRACTION
ALL DISEASE OBSTRUCTION
ALL RECOVERY ELIMINATION

The three obstructions are:
people, habit and food.

Remove your obstruction and
you snap to your goals,
waiting in the wings

FEMALE DUMB DOWN

Why we're going down: They get their views from The View and wise women are very few. Smart: Personal freedom and truth. Dumb: Loyalty to the group. The smart think, the dumb have allegiances. See the hypocrisy within feminism: slowly poison and dumb down into intellectual confusion. The fifties' women were cherished. They knew their place: power behind, enriched and nourished. As society implodes people gang up. We all must work together: false pitch of dividers. Inversions in late democracies: idiots rule while the smart are slaves.

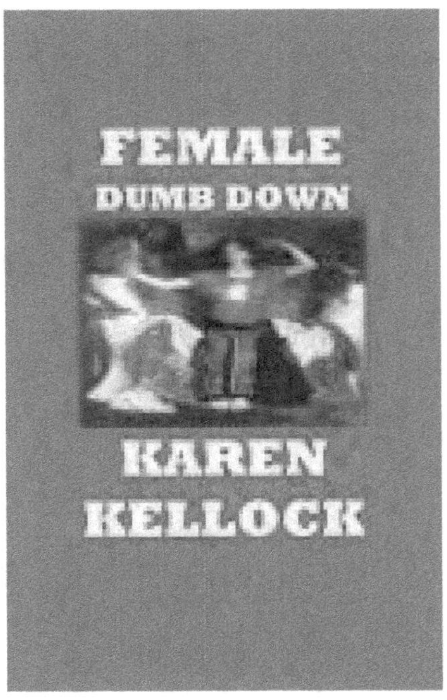

FROM DUMBED TO RENOWNED

FROM DUMBED TO RENOWNED

THE CHOSEN

It shouldn't be this way but this is modernity: First childhood trauma then a life to heal see.

This world today is filled with a bunch of damaged unhealed people: childhood trauma/social evil.

The gaslighting of your greatness starts early, from those closest: family and friends dearest.

They tell you to stay humble or be realistic but in submerging your talents the results are tragic.

It's not good advice but attempt to keep you within boundaries of what THEY comprehend see.

For many of us, we had to burst through the obstructive family before getting to our deserved glory.

Traumatic abuse can bring an implosion of moral boundaries then they all blame you honey.

THE PATH TO HELL: GOOD INTENTIONS

The path to hell is paved with good intentions. You really have to watch those evil helpers son.

Your potential and dreams is what unsettles them. This is why you feel rejected in their presence son.

Society rewards conformity and punishes those daring to be different. Early life was hell going thru this.

The world doesn't appreciate those refusing to fit into it's narrow molds: punished for being bold.

FROM DUMBED TO RENOWNED

Anyone challenging the status quo ruffles feathers & suffers. Breaking through is what matters.

The most dangerous part of gaslighting is how convincing they can be. Self-doubt sets in see.

You shrink your dreams or stay silent when you should be speaking up. I know all about this, yuk!

YOU'RE NOT THE ORDINARY

You start to think you're just like everyone else when you KNOW you're not. I call this inner rot.

The noise from others clouds our inner truth. The world keeps you small, like you're undeserving too.

When you get alone you feel the spark of greatness which they tried to bury. Then you know see.

Your true self is overshadowed by the doubts imposed on you. But they only gaslight threats [you].

You are the light of the world. If you're weren't so great they wouldn't work so hard to doubt your worth.

Tho' they may try, your light can never be extinguished. Accept this truth then embrace your greatness.

The sooner you see these it the sooner you'll become unstoppable. Rest then work on the double.

THEY STRIPPED YOU OF DIGNITY

They stripped you of your dignity, making you feel less than human. I was shocked day & night, moanin'.

They tried to disconnect you from self and the world around you. Calling you deviant/anti-social too.

FROM DUMBED TO RENOWNED

They wanted to break you down so thoroughly you'd be just an empty shell of all you were meant to be.

They didn't just want to hurt you but erase you entirely. You're lucky you escaped but God saved you see.

This is what makes them so sick: true cruelty doesn't just harm but seeks to OBLITERATE: so tragic.

THEY OBLITERATED YOUR IDENTITY

They didn't just target your happiness but aimed at your very identity, making you a despised bug see.

They wanted you to forget who you were and deny your inherent worth which you never deserved!

They treated you like your voice didn't matter and your very existence was of no dam consequence.

This kind of treatment seeks to make you invisible and reduce you to the insignificant [unusable].

Dehumanization begins when no one cares about your pain like crowds loaded onto a prisoner train.

When you're nothing more than a shadow, dehumanization seeps in debasing all you know.

FEELING INSIGNIFICANT IS DIFFICULT

Feeling insignificant is difficult to shake but your great resilience will bring success anyway.

But the light within you--what makes you--could never be extinguished so success remains in full view.

Job was stripped of everything; healthy, wealth and family but his spirit and faith remained steady.

FROM DUMBED TO RENOWNED

Rising from this kind of darkness isn't easy but you did it, a testament to your greatness and destiny.

Your victory is already written in the strength you've shown by continuing to exist, so now REST!

No matter what they threw at you [despite how long your stayed down] you got back up & that's it Sue.

You didn't just survive, you refused to stay broken. No matter how you fell you got back up again.

WHEN SELF-DISGUST RETURNS

Sometimes the old self-disgust returns, a hangover from when they put you down as inferior.

Remind yourself you're CHOSEN [hand-picked] by God and that made em put you down in effect.

Any self-disgust is what THEY laid on you, for you are made in the image of God & chosen like a few.

They put a despicable, disgusting & loathsome image on you and it's hard to extricate from this view.

You really only know someone when they become your enemy. Listen to me, it's a horrible thing to see.

They can't understand you cuz it's not a strength they have. To be under their control cut you in half.

YOU'RE ONLY DEFINED BY RISING AGAIN

Your story is not defined by their actions but your ability to rise again in spite of everything they did man.

Joseph's story shows what they use intended to destroy God uses for something greater to anoint.

FROM DUMBED TO RENOWNED

The story's the same: the more they tried to break you the stronger you became, so no resentments ok?

Resilience in the face of suffering by Paul: "we are hard-pressed on every side but not crushed", aye.

We are persecuted not abandoned, struck down but not destroyed. The past built muscle tho' it annoyed.

SPEAKING TRUTH IS HATE SPEECH?

If we dared speak the truth it was labeled hate speech. Our values fell apart, our goals out of reach.

But now, if we're knocked down we get up again. When resilience is the whole point, we will WIN.

Public humiliation, being betrayed by family or best friends: so what, the point is we get up AGAIN.

Aspiring for greatness: people can relate to this. This is a story for children: from the dregs to success.

There's nothing wrong with being at the BOTTOM and then coming up to the top, hardly forgotten.

President Trump in jail and despised, then Person of the Year and beloved in a giant comeback, aye!

Paul's words are the essence of true resilience: pressed and persecuted but never defeated, yes!

YOUR UNDEFEATABLE STRENGTH

The undefeatable strength within is divine, that's why it is never crushed and comes back up, aye.

Jesus knew the suffering He'd endure but embraced His trials, knowing his greater mission despite all.

FROM DUMBED TO RENOWNED

Your trials have a divine purpose and you too have the strength to overcome them into success.

No matter what they did to crush you, you rise up again showing your true power: that scares em Sue.

The world cannot break divine strength. Being chosen isn't just merely existing, it's totally persevering.

YOUR PRESENCE IS UNSETTLING

Your presence forces them to confront truths about themselves they'd rather ignore [and it's hell]

It's more than they can bare. When they see you they see what they are NOT or will ever be: rare.

Your drive shows their complacency, your courage their degeneracy, your resilience their excuses ok.

Have you ever noticed their strong reaction to your presence tho' you did nothing to bring it on sis?

Your mere existence forces them to reckon with things they'd rather keep hidden [entirely forgotten].

Don't take it personally. It's not about you but what you represent: they can never attain [they can't do it].

Your very existence confronts their comfort zones, making them feel exposed, vulnerable, old.

When enveloped in their darkness it's just easier to project crap onto you then face truths within Sue.

YOUR ENERGY IS MEDICINE TO SOULS

Your energy is medicine to their souls but you feel drained after they go. It's demons of old.

FROM DUMBED TO RENOWNED

You keep bending over backwards for those who would never do the same for you, and it's cruel.

It seems like something's always pulling on you. You must learn to protect your energy too.

The bible says to be ye separate, come out from amongst them ok. God is taking you up & away.

We can't hang with the miserable cuz they drain us. Don't ever think this means you're selfish.

GOD'S GETTING READY

God's getting ready to take you to a whole new level but not if you hangout with the past and the devil.

Every time you're alone you find peace, love, tranquility and optimism. When with others it's lost then.

When I'd leave their presence I got my joy and power back again and it worked immediately man.

People who aren't doing anything want you to do nothing with them. It was awful back then.

IMPORTANT TIPS/WORDS TO WOMEN

Instead of trying to prove your worth, let your presence speak for you and know this comes first.

You step into a space of quiet undeniable magnetism when you master non-verbal communication.

It's not about being seen but becoming someone who naturally draws attention simply by being.

SETTING BOUNDARIES WITHOUT WORDS

Boundaries are set by what you allow or don't allow in your life. How you carry yourself too, aye.

FROM DUMBED TO RENOWNED

You don't have to announce boundaries to make them real. Ex: Don't make plans again if they cancel.

If someone offends with words or actions, don't demand apology just reduce access see.

With time they see your lines not because you've told them but because you've shown them, aye.

WE CONTROL OUR ACTIONS NOT THEIRS

It's. stoicism: we control our OWN actions rather than trying to control others. This works sister.

You can't FORCE them to accept your boundaries but you can enforce them by not tolerating see.

Your silence speaks volume with mistreatment. Not long conversations but pulling away, that's it.

It's not about bottling your emotions but letting your actions do the talking: internal combustion!

Walking away from disrespect/disengaging from drama says "I value myself too much": no trauma.

No manipulation needed: quiet confidence naturally commands respect, especially if you reject.

Boundaries are a form of self-love, teaching others you are WORTHY of their respect and way above.

Boundaries aren't about keeping people out but protecting what's within: that's real clout.

EMBRACE CHANGE WITH GRACE

The subtle shifts, the evolving dynamics: suddenly you feel uncertain and it can be unsettling, tragic.

FROM DUMBED TO RENOWNED

It's tempting to cling to the familiar and fight for things to stay the way they were, to avoid the fear.

The only constant in life is change so don't fight the inevitable but gird up/embrace it after all.

Change is a natural part of every connection and the way you handle it determines character hon'.

He becomes distant. You start to panic but demanding answers just creates friction and adamance.

Acceptance doesn't mean giving up but letting go of your need to control & going with the flow.

GRACE WITH CHANGE SIGNALS STRENGTH

Embracing change with grace signals strength. Adaptability is magnetic: you've got what it takes.

Relationships aren't static, they're living entities evolving with time. They deepen or fade, aye.

Maturity is being willing to let things unfold naturally tho' the outcome's not what you wanted see.

Every change in relationship is opportunity to GROW. Think about this, it's more valuable than you know.

Letting go gives space for something better. Maybe change is not the end but a new beginning sir.

Embracing change isn't easy: it requires PATIENCE and deep trust in yourself to make it through see.

LOVEBOMB CHANGES ARE SHOCKING

People lovebomb on purpose to get you close to them. Change is hard to take with that past forgotten.

FROM DUMBED TO RENOWNED

The narcissist wants to get you to love them a lot so the abuse can start. It's a sick animal with no heart.

When this shift occurs it's totally shocking. It's surreal, you can't believe the words they're using.

You call em out for it & they act like it's nothing. Am I crazy? Your taken for granted world is reeling.

This isn't minor stuff. It's major and despite the apathy of those you talk to, don't take it on the fluff.

MANIPULATIVE, LYING CUNNING

Manipulative, lying, evil, cunning: it's a new generation caught in delusion so don't let it happen.

In this modern era, things are very good then drop off suddenly. This is common and so sad really.

This means we are cooked when it comes to long term. One with your standards who won't squirm?

Earthling's feelings fluctuate constantly. Is this unconditional love truly? Change is reality.

No matter what you must be the best man or woman you can be. That's it: hold steady, stay free.

WEEDING THE FAKE OUT

CHOSEN WOMEN HAVE FEW FRIENDS
A CHOSEN WOMAN IS EXCLUSIVE
LET BAD RELATIONSHIPS GO
SOLITUDE PREPARES FOR BREAKTHROUGH
MORE PRECIOUS THAN RUBIES
YOU DON'T WANNA CROSS A CHOSEN
A WOMAN WHO KNOWS HER WORTH
STOP CHASING AND CREATE SPACE
WHEN YOU WANNA REACH OUT
PEACE COMES FROM THE UNFORCED
QUIET CONFIDENCE IS MOST MAGNETIC
THEY SENSE YOU'RE SPECIAL
WATCH ACTIONS NOT WORDS
INTEGRITY SETS THE STANDARD
TRUTH WILL COME TO LIGHT
STOP HOPING THEY'LL CHANGE

WEEDING THE FAKE OUT

Money: if you have it you'll be finding reasons to spend it but if mature you will not be doing this.

We have to keep focused on the PRIZE in Christ Jesus. Cuz we're almost to the promised land sis.

CHOSEN WOMEN HAVE FEW FRIENDS

There are stumbling blocks in our way: haters and jealous imitators but don't give up sister.

A chosen woman has few friends. This smoothes the way cuz many fail from betrayals of the women.

A chosen women of God walking alone without family, friend or even partner is like none other.

This precious woman of God is to be praised for she is greater and more rare than fine rubies ok.

When a strong independent chosen woman walks alone she's given mind, spirit and body to God alone.

She's not like other women sleeping around with different spirits & surrounded by fake friends.

A CHOSEN WOMAN IS EXCLUSIVE

She doesn't give her time & love to just anyone for it's God's [at a premium] and she's loyal to Him.

A chosen woman even single mothers are so independent they don't need a man, amen.

She doesn't need the praise of other women because she realizes the HATE which is so prevalent.

WEEDING THE FAKE OUT

Women "only have men friends cuz they can't get along with women" but girl you only need HIM, amen.

You don't need your cold family or fake friends cuz you're chosen by the most high God, amen.

A chosen woman walking alone is the most underrated human to walk the planet: misjudged & hated.

It's very rare to find a woman who just walks alone. She just takes good care of her kids and home.

LET BAD RELATIONSHIPS GO

Dear woman if you're in a relationship not doing you any good it's time to let it go, understood?

If hanging with fake friends who are hating on, insecure or jealous of you it's time to let em go sister.

Doom regimen: I held on to fake treacherous girlfriends fearing loneliness if I didn't have them.

She prefers being alone in relationship with God than being with others not HAVING this so solid.

Chosen women walking alone are always crying out to God, praying throughout the day and blessed ok.

All the men try to get her out while the world questions what she's all about but she's seeks no clout.

A chosen woman walking alone is ready/has made room for CHANGE. She looks to the heavens to arrange.

SOLITUDE PREPARES FOR BREAKTHROUGH

This woman in solitude is ready for that breakthrough God promised, that wonderful divine harvest.

WEEDING THE FAKE OUT

Why does she walk alone? She's been through rape and incredible betrayals from family & early home.

She's been taken by men for her finances or body, she knows what it's like to get involved: treachery.

She's been cheated on by many men who told her she was the only one. It's hell out here for moderns.

She needs to be praised, acknowledged and taken care of. It's a hideous image being alone dear ones.

MORE PRECIOUS THAN RUBIES

She is far more precious than fine rubies. The way she carries herself in divine energy & she's clean see.

She knows cleanliness is next to godliness and presents her body as a divine sacrifice not a mess.

She's not like any one you see who will sleep around and waste her time. Every minute is divine.

She's not like the others always gossiping about other women. She is not like any one you've known.

She's not around fake family members when there's no real love there. She'd rather start a new family sir.

When you find a solitary female who's so strong you don't wanna mess with her time, amen.

YOU DON'T WANNA CROSS A CHOSEN

Once she's given her time and energy you don't wanna cross her or you'll see a whole other side sir.

If you come between her and God she will cut you off fast. A chosen in solitude won't take that.

WEEDING THE FAKE OUT

A woman who walks alone with God is very strong. You don't tamper with that so watch out/get along.

Once a man takes her kindness as weakness that's where her scorn comes out: WATCH OUT.

A woman alone is not a lesbian, she's strictly men. She doesn't go for Satan's lies about all this, amen.

A woman walking alone with nobody is one who needs to be praised and "men friends" is not ok.

A woman alone protects her energy at all costs. Also her heart, mind and spirit: there is no loss.

A WOMAN WHO KNOWS HER WORTH

Ladies of the world: unlocking your inner magnetism will astound him in a way that feels genuine.

A woman's entire perspective shifts once she masters the art of NEVER CHASING. Let's dive in darling.

Never chase, always ATTRACT. Never panic when they pull away, the "perfect one" you like like that.

Mistakes maken: You text too much, overcompensate with attention, overfix what feels broken.

Paradox: the more you chase the faster they run. Flip the dynamic: less chase, more you attract.

Enter stoicism: focus on what you can control and what you cannot, let go. You're worth it you know.

You can't control other's feelings but you CAN control how you respond, reclaiming your power see.

You're seeing someone. Suddenly they wane: the dynamic shifts. Don't try harder, step back fast.

WEEDING THE FAKE OUT

Your actions say "my time and energy are valuable. I won't chase if you don't see this at all."

Humans are wired to value what seems scarce. Something too easily available brings disgust.

The available is devalued. It's a psychological phenomenon of humans so don't allow it.

STOP CHASING AND CREATE SPACE

When you stop chasing you create space for him to WONDER and that's the absolute key here.

Make him miss you and reevaluate his own behavior. Chasing works the other way: it's a bummer.

Stoicism uses restraint, patience and composure to quietly shift the dynamic in your favor.

Will stepping back make him lose interest completely? Never if he began genuinely interested see.

If his feeling are real he'll notice and be drawn to self-respect. Through the ages, this is the trick.

If it doesn't work, ask yourself: why'd you want someone who doesn't recognize your value elf?

Stoicism reminds: letting go of someone not serving us makes space for someone better, aye.

How to stop chasing: shift the focus back to yourself. PAUSE when the urge to reach out strikes.

WHEN YOU WANNA REACH OUT

When you wanna reach out, think: does this align with my self-respect? What do I want instead?

WEEDING THE FAKE OUT

It's not about being cold but so magnetic and fulfilled chasing anyone is unnecessary/full of bull.

Attraction isn't about clinging to but being one who others are DRAWN to: remember that Sue.

It's not about him valuing but you starting to value yourself which is so liberating & empowering.

Imagine if you stop chasing entirely: to TRUST that what's meant for you will come naturally.

PEACE COMES FROM THE UNFORCED

Unforced: imagine the peace, confidence and clarity from never chasing but simply ATTRACTING!

Know your worth like a rare gem. Do you know your true value or letting the world define it friend?

Measuring self worth through outer validation is a TRAP: like beauty standards or social media crap.

Your worth is not up for negotiation. No one can grant it nor take it away, that's what I've learned son.

It simply IS. Imagine yourself as a rare gem stone. If it is unseen, is it less valuable when shown?

It's value remains unwavering and undeniable whether it is noticed or not. The world's view is rot.

Knowing your worth regardless of their view is the most magnetic of all traits you could have Sue.

QUIET CONFIDENCE IS MOST MAGNETIC

It's not about arrogance or boasting but moving through life with quiet confidence for all to see.

WEEDING THE FAKE OUT

Unshakable self-respect changes everything like how you interact with men and boundary setting.

Self-respect changes how people perceive and treat you. This is the most important thing Sue.

Humans sense you're not just anyone. You're one deserving respect, a true lady never to shun.

When you truly value yourself it changes everything, like how you interact with men. It's alluring friend.

Self-respect determines how you set boundaries and how others treat you--not to overstep too.

THEY SENSE YOU'RE SPECIAL

People sense you're not just anyone. You're the rare one who deserves respect for it's what you expect.

Self-reflection builds this respect. Are you kind, humane, considerate? Use these questions for it.

Use such self-reflection rather than external validation. This builds strength in the face of put-downs.

When you operate from a place of self-worth you stop tolerating poor treatment: that's allure.

When you're too self-respectful to settle for anything less, others will pickup on this energy sis.

People will see you're not one needing to beg for attention or approval, you're just great that's all.

Be one who chooses relationships aligning with your values not insecurities. Get over that sweetie.

The way you see yourself sets the tone for how others see you. It's magnetism through and through.

WEEDING THE FAKE OUT

This isn't just theory but a law of human dynamics. It's dark stoic psychology and rings fabulous.

By self-respect you teach and raise the standards of those around you. It's how you control em Sue.

What makes you unique? What qualities set you apart? Take a moment to reflect on these for a start.

When you truly see your value all interactions will shift. What an insight solving all rifts!

WATCH ACTIONS NOT WORDS

Watch actions, not words. By observing just actions you protect your emotional well being girls.

They promise the world but can't even deliver simple gestures of care. Things don't match up sir.

Consistency in action reveals commitment while their inconsistency shows the lack of it.

It's not about expecting perfection but watching for patterns, for they tell ALL about everyone.

All they say is how much they love/care about you but they don't show up when you need em Sue.

Do they come up with excuses or worse: altogether forget their words? This is the gist girls.

Instead of reacting emotionally to every word, maturity learns to step back and WATCH, observe.

The over-use of "I love you" is a buzzword trap. These are the ones you have to watch mostly: fact.

Don't confront every little slip up, but quietly take note and file it away. Then pull back & don't trust ok.

WEEDING THE FAKE OUT

Adopting this mindset allows you to see people for who they are not what you wish or they play you for.

This is being grounded in REALITY, not caught up in the whirlwind of words that hypnotizes girls.

It builds self-awareness too. Are your. actions lining up with your values? Are you who you say Sue?

INTEGRITY SETS THE STANDARD

Being in full integrity with your values sets the standards for both you and others too.

Do they follow thru on commitments? Do they show you care/respect even when inconvenient for them?

Their actions speak louder than their words ever could. It's about protecting your heart, understood?

Prioritizing actions over words reduces the risk of being swept up into false promises which HURT.

You're creating space for REAL relationships based on trust, RELIABILITY and mutual respect at last.

People always reveal their true selves in time. Save yourself a world of hurt by watching, aye.

Don't rush to conclusions or force things to happen. Just be watchful with things not forgotten.

TRUTH WILL COME TO LIGHT

Trust that the truth will come to light and always respond with grace and wisdom, alright?

Truth is about alignment: if people's actions line up with who they claim to be then you'll be OK see.

WEEDING THE FAKE OUT

Living by this standard you naturally attract those with integrity. It's a silent thing, always works for me.

Are you paying attention to actions or getting lost in words? This is how you judge yourself girls.

When you focus on things REAL you step into a place of strength. It's a magic trick about people I think.

It becomes easy on the internet, since that is ALL WORDS. You easily separate the two worlds.

STOP HOPING THEY'LL CHANGE

You stop hoping someone will change and easily recognize who they are RIGHT NOW ok.

Starting with that place of clarity you make decisions that honor your worth and life becomes easy.

By focusing on actions not words you take control of emotional experience which is crucial for us.

Never again to give your power away to empty promises. That's the old life of painful experiences.

You now invest in powerful relationships that are as real as they feel. Fakers & losers are gone, sealed.

It's worth the wait for true respect and connection. It speeds it up by eliminating fakers & bums.

FEMALE DUMB DOWN

For years I took on and acted out the scripts they laid on me thru vile projection, an automaton.

I had to produce or the Dunning-Krugers around me woulda targeted and locked me in.

Long after repentance the shame can remain. This is where Jesus comes in, He erases it ok?

I'm no longer hurt when they censor me cuz it's probably a woman who can't think & hates novelty.

If not an overt racist you're a covert racist which cannot be seen, proven nor disproven just assumed.

A 50 year project finally visible at 45 years--long time to endure misjudgment from kin and peers.

PRODUCE FOR IDENTITY

I had to produce to buttress up my grandiose self-image: "delusions of grandeur" sister said.

Your social devices show extreme insecurity & I wish you'd stop doing it, it's embarrassing you twit.

What is Dunning-Kruger? Dumb people thinking they're smart. It's the whole problem, be separate.

It doesn't matter how hard you worked on it so stop saying it. The point is does it work?

Modern women get off on their titles, accolades, good reviews, social contacts, likes and the like.

Your work is done, time for music. This reroutes the brainwaves with new grooves and I love it.

FEMALE DUMB DOWN

You're under God's hand until He decides to reveal you--no longer hidden under a bushel.

The system wants to minimize and shrink the woman but with godly transformation she EXPANDS.

They had me so boxed in with nonverbal put-downs I shrank down to nothing/dumbed/meltdown.

I'd get big and the system would squash me down. Before maturity it was recurrent: meltdown.

Social devices to make her conform are immediate and unconscious--can she overcome all of it?

If not insults from inferior men she shouldn't be around, it's the nonverbal devices dragging her down.

SHRINKING IDENTITY IN SYSTEMS

They wanna shrink, collapse, lock her in. That's society but God wants her expansive transformation.

He expands her at first but after discard slowly starts to tear her down and the poor dear conforms.

It's queen consciousness vs. a mindset established by the outside world that constricts/shrinks girls.

Sucking up to some guy you shouldn't even be around: a loser who triggered that old trauma bond.

I can forgive you but it sure was a hard life for me when you chose them instead: it was treachery.

I could be so BIG when alone--happy & individualized--then sink down to hell when they came around.

Alone with my husband I was a queen but surrounded by them was a new regime--sullen and mean.

FEMALE DUMB DOWN

Queen consciousness is the opposite to social consciousness and Jimmy went along with it.

Just as we left our blissful solitude he melted in with the multitudes and saw me differently dude.

As he succumbed and I lost my bloom he went in with the social women, easily bribed from then on.

Beaten up psychologically as self-esteem goes to hell and self-disgust: that's the system sis.

And here there's another loser thinking he's superior to her, tearing her down but I see you sir.

The minute there's a breakup the women take charge, officiously involved to finish the job.

HOOKED BY LOSERS

And here there's another dam loser you're attracted to, an attachment bond trigger and a miser.

Cuz the others put me in disdain he changed his mind. Then I started begging, that's the system.

Because the others saw me negatively he saw me differently--it's called social psychology.

When I went to the first dinner to meet my new neighbors I walked into a buzz saw--that's it forever.

Being single sux but living in a narrow universe controlled by anger is worse—being homesick for Self.

The victim becomes cruel herself. She wakes up to this reality years later and then she's well.

At this .point she can either lay down and be weak or stand up and be strong. Addictions begin.

FEMALE DUMB DOWN

I lost all my bloom and looked like doom. I forgot how far I'd fallen/sunk in swill from that day on.

With divorce she stuck her head in the frig and never came out. FAST: do the exact opposite.

I get the vibe they hate women around here. Hell if I'm leaving home unescorted by you dear.

The woman is supposed to be the BLESSING for a man not disdained and treated like a doormat.

In a blind fog of denial, the queen becomes cruel and doesn't realize it till later and the truth.

When around him I feel an undertow. He brings up the past or gossip and that's all I need to know.

This is how weak I was: They didn't know me, it was pure projection and I bought it--I took it on!

Renaissance was a sudden uprush of creativity in an entire generation, a surge of new visions.

We have a right to change our mind. Stop calling it fickle, the problem is foolishly sticking behind.

Instead of doing his work he becomes contumacious: always rebelling against authority, a mess.

What scared the women most was being seen as subhuman, treated like a piece of meat.

A realization that no one cares changes behavior. Brazen misconduct was ok with mom but not here.

SOLUTION: AUTOPHAGY ON CHEATERS

/fast and separate

FEMALE DUMB DOWN

I celebrate those who make a success of their lives not play victim.

The left is now like cornered rats willing to fight on to the end.

Democrats want voters so it's Islam and feminists: a cold-blooded alliance.

Feminists end the discussion when it comes to empowering women and part of that is accepting Islam.

Though the left lost they still want victory so bad they lie, make things up, assert nonsense nonstop.

Antifa: Anyone who's conservative is a Nazi and should be punished.

What choice do we have other than to defend ourselves?

They hate Alex Jones cuz the plan was if Hillary won he'd be shut down but instead now he's renowned.

They love Hillary cuz she's female--it's reflected glory: "it's about women". How stupid, amen?

Why we're going down: They get their views from The View. The wise women are very few.

For those of you who have experienced what it's like to be under female tyranny, I have affinity.

Don't focus on people (filthy rags). They'll always fail you so let Jesus be everything and forgive scumbags.

One member's cruel rejection turns out positively as we reject the whole darn crew as gossipy.

Decency not diversity is our strength.

FEMALE DUMB DOWN

Let the Assassination Movement supercharge the populist-patriot movement of superior men.

The level of media falsehood is like nothing we've ever seen, beyond North Korea and commie fiends.

Don't panic with the rise of the inferior, as good men come forward (as we've seen all through history).

We the patriotic Americans face the Muslim hordes with the communists as they attack U.S. citizens.

If they hate Trump after all the good he's done in so little time drop 'em they're not worth a dime.

"Trump said this, Trump said that"--they don't know what to do cuz he's REAL so they plan to kill him flat.

Can't pull out of the system admitting they were conned.

Smart: Personal freedom and truth. Dumb: Loyalty to the group

There's gotta be a cutoff--closure: When you give up cuz it can't go on forever and now it's in your favor.

There comes a point where you make the decision--their time is all spent--and you won't relent.

The fifties' women were cherished. They knew their place: power behind, enriched and nourished.

"Can't we all just get along? We all must work together"—Yah, right: false pitch of dividers.

FEMALE DUMB DOWN

They look so happy in their similarity but it's just a human system hating anomalies and that's you, baby.

It's the media creating the kill-Trump thing: they create reality for the finks.

Inversions in late democracies: idiots rule and smart are slaves.

See the hypocrisy within feminism and you'll drop the feminist label, ma'am.

As society implodes people gang up. Everyone talking like ganstas--just shut up and board up!

O-Care makes no sense unless to ruin us with terror and suspense. It's crazy not just tense.

I am watching a nation going down, not up. The only thing giving us hope is Donald Trump.

Before we knew better liberals were just a fetter but after repentance it's a different story altogether.

Slowly poison, dumb down and confuse intellectually. That's how the elites have done this actually.

Hillary's corruption is so massive it's historic like Hitler. It's almost too big to contemplate but most hate her.

Cognitive Dissonance (the gist): To maintain our worldview we reject all discrepant evidence.

Racist: One who wins an argument with a liberal.

The smart think, the dumb have allegiances.

Unable to handle the disappointment of losing they have lost their minds, truly.

Hillary meant a certain decline, a drop to the bottom in a nosedive. Unlike her this is no lie.

Liberals are so dumbed/messed up they hate the man who can turn it all around and fix it like the Brexit.

How dare Trump bring millions of new jobs to America.

Men have all the power, women don't make the same money: all this is feminist training/men shaming.

Hillary says it's ok to kill babies right before delivery. This woman is a sadist and ok with the despicably gory.

Women hire attorneys to ruin men's lives: it's now cultural to male-despise.

The deep state is planning an assassination and desensitizing the public to the imminent destruction.

For the first time our country is controlled by evil, wicked traitors and destroyers.

It's the spirit of lawlessness in the Last Days. It is so horrible when they think crime pays.

The further a society drifts from truth the more it will hate those who speak it. George Orwell

Google: War is peace, freedom is slavery, diversity is uniformity.

Progressivism 2017: Putting people on lists for having wrong political viewpoints and firing em.

FEMALE DUMB DOWN

The four biggest insanity-producers are food, alcohol, pharma and people--and all four can be evil.

The point of one meal a day is every day you're better--a little cleaner/leaner with more digestive fire.

God and diet is all that matters. The saints choose beauty to compensate for these evil days, the latter.

The healthier we get the more body rejects bad food. Bubbles, acid, dizziness and burping--not cool.

Goodbye food, hello body--cuz it bloats, dries, gets flaky. It reacts through distortion so watch it baby.

In all day fasts, seek higher elements. A balmy breeze, feeling of sun on the skin, the stars, amen.

Tubby gained 100 pounds then learned how to stay thin right: one meal and no more downs.

Desire to be a model (an exemplar of the best human specimens) at the highest peak--are you able?

How boring if you're not eating what you need cuz you're constraining to a theory--how dreary.

Though it's not on your diet it's maybe something you need. Do not be a robot with your food, be freed.

When you finally get rid of all dieting materials you'll be free and health will return with normal meals.

Autophagy: How fasting helps the body cleanse Itself, replacing cells and de-aging into an elf.

FEMALE DUMB DOWN

Answer to all problems: fast and pray daily. You do that by eating one meal only: Now life is gravy.

The true artist loses all the weight by his own instincts not what the others say--elastic and thin, ok?

Be like a snake: free the mind. Eat then don't eat for fat-burning consciousness and being refined.

Lose all the weight than autophagy will eat the bad cells/loose skin and replace with good ones, ok?

Wait as long as you can for your one meal, lest you must eat again and victory won't be a steal.

Life began when I gave up diets: I saw they were All legit by science but hijacked life like pirates.

Things are best six hours into the daily fast: in energy, clarity and appearance you'll be having a blast.

Fast the way you want to, tell em to shut up. Everyone's an expert but the True Self's a magic elf.

There's truth on both sides so I like to Reversal Diet. When I get sick of one I do the other--I even fry it.

To get "the look" you gotta activate youthifier: human growth hormone: Fast and work til tired to the bone.

People object to Reversal Diet. They want you to go one or the other, not have fun with life (truly live it).

Church dieting is a demonic agenda.

FEMALE DUMB DOWN

By getting away from facebook tension, I lost weight. It was too much anxiety and a burden, changing fate.

Food automatically makes us fat so we gotta compensate for that: skinny for longevity--daily fast.

Living in the past is like toxic gas. All variables have changed so be vindicated by a fast.

Eat then don't eat, let the fasting process take over. Fast for the day for a complete makeover.

It's not so much what you eat but how long you fast in between meals: fast and all diseases are healed.

The efficacy of fasting surpasses what you eat, so eat what you want then fast and don't cheat.

Acid comes from bad food you're fed, then it's Rolaids, Alka-Seltzer, milk, bread. Stop pain: fast instead.

Orthorexia: constraining food choices to dogma rather than what you want or need--dangerous, indeed!

I eat what I want when I want and that's my new diet. I'm through with gurus who even lie about it.

Sinners have a muddy aura. This includes bad food sins making one pasty and bloated: horror!

What you should eat is not a diet, it's what's available, what works, what tastes good/no fireworks.

Eternal consciousness: get outa the temporal

FEMALE DUMB DOWN

True culture is about intrigue, lust for knowledge and appreciation of beauty--not this trashy tragedy.

They have nothing, it's just this that defines them.

Violent delights have violent ends. Shakespeare

Plays. Once they're desensitized they get ideas to kill their leader: the normalizing of political violence.

Finally a real strong leader comes around and they hate him, but we the people want him.

This new line "bullying" is created to divide us and it's magnified in youth--see how they lied to us too.

Mental illness is rising with the youth. Is it any wonder, being taught lies/how to be uncouth?

Left interprets free speech of conservatives as violent and violence of the left as free speech.

They attacked Sarah Palin for the same reason: She was real, emphatic, family loving, pleasing.

The worst thing about liberals is how "good" they are. But look what they condone--perversion not just war.

Antifas wear masks, carry weapons, block speaking and use intimidation to cow people into silence.

Modern movies: sex and effects.

Villains always reorganize and come back.

FEMALE DUMB DOWN

Just living in a shack brings more abuse, cuz it all fits--everything fits--even the booze.

The greater your potential the more they try to getcha.

Individual = freedom. Group = tyranny. Christianity is the individual not the false church of many.

An old woman always for abortion now faces death panels by the same eugenics without option.

If you have the wrong politics that annoys they'll do anything to you regardless of how it destroys.

Everything with liberals is that peer pressure: You aren't cool cuz they weren't cool in school.

Left took over politics when we weren't looking. We were complacent but now awake and kicking.

The state of the union is dismal. That's all denied by evil but known by the people (who stay cheerful).

Suddenly their liberal rants seemed pure static. Then it was easy to ignore these dumb leftist fanatics.

Liberals won't face facts. They just "know what they know" and make stuff up--give em the axe.

We've reached a point where patriotism is actually frowned upon--freedom is truly under the gun.

Mobs turn good kids into bad ones--warped by the crowd mentality--but America is individuality.

FEMALE DUMB DOWN

Global warming/climate change: Shut up and believe.

This world project was a 100 trillion per decade carbon tax and Trump said "No" cuz he had the facts.

As the Antarctic gets larger they tell school children they've all fallen and Hollywood fakes are all-in.

Our world is run by imperious gangsters. To them we're like useless eaters or laboratory hamsters.

Most have no idea what globalism means. It's the bleakest common denominator as it's all run by fiends.

The world looks on in sadness as we endure the utter madness.

Ban all countries who throw gays off buildings or marry children.

Contradictions, lies and a dumbed down public: Islamaphobic self-censure spreads ISIS like wildfire.

Liberals are just pawns in a global scheme of tyranny by destroying us and our freedoms completely.

Religious vs. atheists always had a difference of opinion but at least they were civil--we've sunk to a new low.

Most dangerous Muslim is not maniac but the guy with a suit and tie saying not all Muslims are like that.

It's all designed to wreck the country and fold us into global government. Americans see this, amen.

FEMALE DUMB DOWN

CNN, the NYT and Washington Post IS ISIS: they are enemies of our president and makers of these crises.

A civil war as patriots tried to take America back--the enraged left wanted Clinton after Barrack.

The democrats are terrorists: They're the enemy, they called for this.

The radical left is allied with Islam cuz they see it as their muscle: bam!

Government's a dangerous master as they jail the pastors and anyone else trying to divert disaster.

They hate Trump cuz he's a strong leader in the real world. Liberals are utopians only: weird.

The anti-Trumps get nit-picky. They can't stand anything breaking with the old matrix or the hippies.

Anyone real with common sense is viciously attacked. It was a relief for me to realize this, in fact.

Cultural sickness affects people like hypnosis. Without a strong foundation in the Lord it's like osmosis.

Stockholm Syndrome: apt title for the region. Self-destruction--whatever could have happened?

Madness of the German people as country crumbles: wives and children are violated but no mumbles.

Disarming Americans while arming our enemies is treason. See how serious this really is, please hon'.

FEMALE DUMB DOWN

Trump came to end political correctness and identity politics.

Those that are dead see the living as a curse.

Left's aligned with Islam to flood it's enemies with death and mayhem.

The fact Trump has such a high rating of 50% despite all the media's trying to do: must be destiny!

We are forced to fund the propaganda aiming to undue the society we love.

These are sick brats and babies: emotionally brittle and mentally ill as the result of Marxism instilled.

if voters don't get a handle on what's happening we're going into hell and we won't be laughing.

Idiotic liberal women--feminists--use their power to punish people and it's very lawless and evil.

Main Media: presstitutes, decepticons, collaborators, propagandists, fraudsters, arrogant scum.

They have an inverted sense of self-worth compelling destruction of anything countering them (truth).

By failing to prepare you're preparing to fail. Ben Franklin

The New Age won't judge a thing. it's all good they say but what happens when faced with reality?

Creativity saves me from fright or the doldrums. It's my own thing man: down with news by bums.

Look at the facts then make a decision, not agenda-driven.

Through Trump we avoided the profiteers of doom. God loves drunks, children and America too.

Don't let em invade your privacy for that's the most important thing to freedom lovers, see?

Russia wants to join the west in prosperity but keep her identity. She came outa communism/she's free.

Trump will go down in history as the most wildly hated politician because he delivered on his promises.

The Washington Post is a liberal smear machine.

Government won't focus on jobs for returning veterans just illegal aliens so it's gonna be bad until heaven.

Often liberals hate conservatives: banned, censored, dis-invited, ostracized and ruined with out apologies.

They think they're smart but no liberal is. This isn't the party of JFK--it's lewd, lying and communist.

These liberals in control are extremely affluent from treacherous deals and thus have great appeal.

They lost the elections, they miscalculated and can't get over it so now it's an assassination spirit.

Misreading data by generalizations which are agenda driven.

If you're gonna tell a lie tell it often until it is believed and make it a big one too, that's their rule.

FEMALE DUMB DOWN

Sexualized Rot: We're forced to accept it's normalization as if it's an accepted fact—it is not.

The coddled left condemns "micro-aggressions" and "trigger warnings" so be clever, be deft.

They don't even know how to think but these angry spoiled rotten children seek to make a stink.

The Hijab has become the symbol of resistance in the age of Trump to feminists.

Social engineers are setting themselves up as the new priesthood, telling us 100 genders is good.

Veganism can be a leftist tomb. They care more about a pig then a little baby killed in the womb.

These sick brats are the magnified reflection of the old hippies who raised them with NO sense of sin.

They say Caitlin Jenner is "stunning and brave" while vets who died are forgotten in the grave.

Huma is Hillary's lover married to Weiner. The lascivious left thinks nothing of such things inferior.

Depending on how empty one is (most are) they absorb the cultural neurosis, morally below par.

Your work is to fill your mind with good things. Mayberry, the Cartrights--old ones with morals, not finks.

Have your standards dropped so low you actually go along with this/can't see it's from hell below?

One digestive burn a day, that's all I can take. Eat again and feel miserable the next day--big mistake.

I even get acid after water. Eat then Don't Eat for 24 hours--no more acid pain and you'll be hotter.

Fast food causes cancer and obesity--very dangerous, so avoid hunger by eating a big breakfast.

When you go to stores you see the dead, dying and mutated. Not just dumb but fat and constipated.

Most big breasts are boob-fat from bad food. 1950's actresses had small ones/weren't crude.

"Lunch with little, sup with less--better yet, go to bed supperless"--advice to patriots by Ben Franklin.

I'd only eat once a day, since digestion robs creativity. Make yourself ready for the cue, with levity.

In the depression people ate less and found they got healthier. Elimination makes one happier.

Eat in a six hour window then fast 18 hours a day and this is what I call the magic carpet and perfect days.

I can't control the outer so will focus on the inner world and that means diet/fasting is the pearl.

Every diet will work for some people. But not all and that's the point: for some the results are evil.

Just get some rice noodles and soy sauce, the rest of the meal comes from your greenhouse.

FEMALE DUMB DOWN

It's anorexogenic but great: Give up on the outer/uncontrollable, control the body and the mind follows.

It's how they look that makes me want/not want their books. If no looks it's a diet scam of crooks.

Every good veterinarian ascertains the health of the animal by it's looks: Duh, obvious isn't it, kooks?

You gotta lift your face without surgery. That's through the food and when you do that the Face Lift is free.

I hit my best combining the best of seven theories. Don't ever follow just one or it's tyranny.

After 40 you gotta work at being handsome/pretty. You can't take it for granted but achieve it and be steady.

A blood filled with crap (food/air contaminants) shows in bloat, mud tones, pastiness, lines and disfigurement.

Beauty is: lack of obstruction. It's who we are (God's image) when free of dirty/worldly contamination.

It's not fat it's bloat cuz you ate the wrong type. Now just switch back to God's and it cleans the pipes.

A blood free of all toxins is called genetic body fluids and this creates God's beauty with words lucid.

Deceiving spirits/doctrines of demons concerning diet: even churches advance it but better to wing it.

Diets are men's inventions not according to Christ: we are complete in Him/only He can suffice.

FEMALE DUMB DOWN

Drill down: they don't know what they're talking about. Tragic, violent clowns.

Lady what you said sounds like something from "The View". You're smarter than that, aren't you?

Even if no one's shaming them they still feel shamed so push things further (get Christians framed).

The established authorities are liberal feminists who are all for Hillary and other such chicanery.

All of their problems will magically go away if I will just pretend they are the sex they claim.

These sick brats and old hippies are sexual anarchists and communists. If they're in control we're finished.

Race-pimping is a trillion dollar business of liberalism, ok? PC zombies have become Maoists today.

Called the most beautiful city in the world, San Francisco's smeared with feces because liberals rule.

We're programmed by the artificial culture, a fake. It's dirty, it's nasty and I've had all I can take.

You went that way cuz the schools deliberately misled you. Now you're all puffed up, bloated, suicidal.

God's wrath comes in many forms but when coming to nations, scary unpredictability is the norm.

Drones and robots are what they've got. The message: you're automatically caught and it'll hurt a lot.

FEMALE DUMB DOWN

Women cry rape but campuses are the safest place.

Where are the sweet little ladies? They're busy but few are tidy.

Women have seriously slipped into promiscuity but being a slut only brings terrible depression, truly.

The only way to fill the void is with someone who truly cares: duh.

Why marriage is simple: An authentic unbreakable connection with another human brings contentment.

If a feminist really wants to help women, why would she join forces with Islam or those with the bomb?

Liberals unite with Muslims becuz the "enemy of my enemy is my friend". Who is their enemy? Christians, man.

They're the walking dead being propped up artificially but with the public they have no legitimacy.

Only a radical communist would try to destroy America. These types also lie while acting like angelica.

Women degrade husbands publically like they see on TV: a plan to degrade West taken over globally.

If you act like a lady you won't have to go through nearly as much, like being taken to lunch.

A thought that sometimes makes me crazy: Am I, or are the others crazy? Albert Einstein

Most admired trait: bouncing back from all their B.S.!

FEMALE DUMB DOWN

One little insight, one tiny hunch, one slight change is enough to flip you into total success, outa this mess.

Ok so I went wild: I had a moment. But it's not constant, nor a habit.

I cherish my routine so don't come without calling, I get mean.

To overcome loneliness I lived alone in a cabin on one thousand acres of nature. 20 years relying on God, I matured.

Stop hankering over things that can never be. Give your love and attention to others who value thee

Getting rid of people is like a boulder taken out of your eye. They eclipsed you, so say bye-bye!

After being a worm in their eyes I'm super-ambitious. All behavior is compensatory with results auspicious.

Sin keeps you longer and costs more than you thought. Repent and forget all you've been taught.

Finally, an event-thought-change and you snap into breakthrough and to the past, pooh-pooh.

Low IQ people are highly social/have allegiances. High IQ people are careful/don't take chances.

High IQ people aren't comfortable with networks, dates, social frivolities--but low IQs love these miseries.

Superior man has a few friends for life. Lower man sees strength in numbers so the social is rife.

Smart people think, dumb people have allegiances.

Must sacrifice your own religion, cultural identity, traditions and morals or leave the EU: horrible.

Globalist elite for open-door migration will crush the people: prediction.

"If these fuddy-duddies can't let go of their local roots and Christian heritage let's replace em."

It's about the erosion of the nation state, conformity and never stepping out of line: that's EU today.

It's a gang of thugs and strong-arms aiming to intimidate to get their way and you should be alarmed.

San Diego schools are promoting the radical anti-American ideology called Islam. Share this, tell em.

Anti-Islamaphobia campaigns favor Islam over other religions. It's one or the other, no contradictions.

The Travel Ban is logical, sensible and reasonable.

Under the global anti-colonial model, even our poor are rich enough to pay the tax which would level.

The socially regressive attitudes of Muslims in the west are horrifying. Calling it "moderate" is like lying.

If you speak against Islam, globalism or Hillary Clinton we'll find you with GPS to your front door ma'am.

Standing up to a murderous regime with no respect for human life is more important than anything else.

FEMALE DUMB DOWN

Fake news: If they told the truth they'd be fired so they're stuck in globalist lies, the muck and mire.

They can't think. Blocked by tyranny and trance, from debate they shrink. Driven to the brink, they drink.

Prepare for shocks! 2018 shows extremes you've never seen as your world rocks. Hide: sly as a fox.

Old hippies like Hillary don't think they should be honest. That virtue's been erased the longest.

FOX News: Just by debating it (what should be obvious) they're minimizing it so I'm rejecting it.

The masochist Germans will go along with any horrible thing as long as not accused of wrongthink.

The Murdock boys (FOX) are very liberal and wife is a friend of Hillary. Forget Fox and just do independent study.

Don't call Barry "president" he was destroyer, the closer of 100-year plan now back as annoyer/badman.

It hurts being betrayed by liberals but when it's your own family it's worse than vicious animals.

People are afraid of silence--that must be it--so they fill it up with erratic nonsense to feel legit.

50 year false paradigm intervened--creating fiends, men/women mean--but Trump made us free.

To feel good about yourself, focus on how dumb they are--see this difference to be a star.

FEMALE DUMB DOWN

Cultural Marxism and feminism undermined masculine self-confidence so men are in confusion.

The feelings, behaviors and characteristics of masculinity for centuries are now sexist and malevolent.

Moral relativism and hedonistic nihilism of the 90's created neuroticism.

Neomasculinity is adaptation to the created feminist reality.

Neomasculinity is about buffering up attractiveness to get women, rather than hard work/it's leaven

Trump: may get our traditions back in a hurry. Hillary: most despotic regime in our history.

The love of liberty is the love of others; the love of power is the love of ourselves. William Hazlitt

Oppose with manly firmness any invasions on the rights of the people. Thomas Jefferson

You have not converted a man because you have silenced him. John Morley

The price of apathy towards public affairs is to be ruled by evil men. Plato

The lower the IQ the tighter their group. The higher the IQ the more the individual seeks the truth.

Man is born free, and everywhere he is in chains. Rousseau

The Stockholm Syndrome is a suckup to the oppressor and it's as bad as the cuckholder, yes sir.

FEMALE DUMB DOWN

If you don't wanna die that way, don't eat what they eat. Look how they age/get sick--eat right, don't cheat.

A clean toxin-free body is the foundation of true health. We feel so good after cleaning cells from filth.

Digestion is a big issue, because if it doesn't digest right it dulls your spirit and ruins your whole life.

Fasting is a flight off into the clouds, angels, ancestors, foreverness and on earth: cleverness.

You get to a point where digestion causes gas, belching, acid, bubbles, feels like cement: troubles.

Most food is poison and noxious deadly chemicals are everywhere. But who believes this, who's in despair?

Supposedly the GMO and pesticides etc. won't have an effect if I pray over it but that's hard to accept.

When you get to a point where digestion is hell, may I suggest smoothies: improves looks and smells.

You get to a point where digestion feels like a brick in the gut. Mental energy goes down/you're in a rut.

Digestion robs creativity. It's a budget: the less goes here, the more goes there-- productivity.

Whether pain or weight gain I know what it's like to feel trapped in a body you hate but there is a way.

85% of Americans are obese (BMI >23)

FEMALE DUMB DOWN

 **Globalism is forced austerity = America no longer a rarity.**

Globalism's meant to make us poor, dummy. That's why Hollywood's such a joke but never funny.

Paris Agreement Lies: "The earth will be in the balance, the seas will rise, the polar bears will all die."

They never tell you about the carbon tax, it's always about the polar bears, like you're five year old kids.

"All cultures are equal"--what a bunch of bull but readily accepted by those on drugs medical.

Stop preaching women's rights and focus only on culture, language and borders--all that matters.

They're not escaping war they're running to money. These are economic immigrants, honey.

Raping children in swimming pools is just a cultural mistake but never feign Nazi salute in Germany, no way.

An unemployable army of young angry men making their country unendurable, a torture den.

Who gains from all this mass immigration? BIG government, BIG business and BIG religion.

It's babble in the bible: get us so confused with other languages, cultures and evil fables.

We have to compensate for what was done to us by insane Hussein--that means don't let any more in.

FEMALE DUMB DOWN

 **Today's feminism is a mental illness since it's radical Islam it endorses.**

Economic migrants are not fleeing war zones.

"The EU is great--it's the bastion of tolerance and liberalism" they're told as they are so miserable.

What is the benefit of uneducated third world cultures flowing in--what do the People get out of em?

Debt is a form of global redistribution (note owned by Saudis etc) and that's what Obama gave em.

Who profits from illegal immigrant surge: Look it up--they're making a mint from this scourge.

FOX doesn't care nor talk about illegal immigration--ever notice this? In news it's a lie to omit.

We've been invaded and we must fight back. Read Government Zero today on the rack.

Obama and Merkel were invading their own nations to crush out everything good from tradition.

Nazi Guilt: They see Syrians running to money as if they're Jews running from gas chambers—loony.

Celebrate your future where ethnic Germans will be minorities in their own communities: Whee!

Germans either speak out now as your culture dissolves or leave as nothing else possibly solves.

FEMALE DUMB DOWN

 She has made feminists look so stupid. Good.

She chops off his head then says he's a bully who should apologize instead.

They destroy all that we create. Or they make destructive, black arts while wanting to dictate.

Left-loving celebrities defending the plastic bubble they live in.

When faced with questions they never answer just attack Trump.

Goes to their head, can't stay straight. They always fold though ugly neuroses may come late.

How irrelevant they are yet ego blinds them to this fact. It's embarrassing: a classless act.

In the past they knew women belonged in the home but now they're expected to leave and roam.

The religious life is an inner journey, not an outer one. Social doesn't mean good, hon'.

If truth is a menace and logic a crime, can you really be a great and loyal friend of mine?

Less intelligent people rate their abilities highly and don't realize their inept inferiority. Dunning-Kruger Effect

People who are bad at stuff think everything is easy. Dunning Kruger

Smarter people tend to be filled with self-doubt because they know how much they don't know.

Anti-God LGBT philosophy from pit of hell.

FEMALE DUMB DOWN

Feminism makes "housework" a dirty word, despite it being more important than all other work.

The liberal acts like he's the aristocrat/you're the barbarian. But inside he's the lawless one, condoning sin.

That's not her, it's the world in her. She's too permeable--with boundaries down she loses her demur.

There's a connection between sex sin and poverty: Thus the nation's going broke, predictably.

Constantly on the lookout for a better option instead of committing to the nice guy.

Relation of poverty to sex sin: Of course it doesn't always work that way--look at Bill Clinton.

Neomasculine men won't stay with Cultural Marxists who are more likely to cheat.

You said I "hurt you"--liberals always turn it around, don't they? It was you who did me in, but hey...

Kids need nurturing, intellectually forceful, emotionally strong parents so the state prevents that.

Because they put you down you forgot who you are. You're a star but seen as bizarre.

Sex is a biological fact but "gender" is a sociological construct and we're sick of all that: YUK.

FEMALE DUMB DOWN

We shouldn't care about mean words from those we don't respect. Ignore little people/stiff necks.

According to the press it's the conservative's fault about the shooting: we created the mess.

We must now quickly act bold in civil disobedience to denounce the rise of liberal terrorism.

They protest patriarchy, white supremacy and capitalism but when they talk they have little to say.

Age has nothing to do with maturity.

That's all they know, that's all they care to know, so: Give up on them, time isn't yours to blow.

I've finally gone past the trivia and surface media. I see the larger picture so can relax into musica.

You wouldn't be hating em unless God hates em too. Wait and see: divine vindication's coming to you!

When God decides to punish you, wow. When God decides to reward and bless you, wow, wow, wow.

You're infinitely worse than you think you are, but God's grace is even greater so now be a star!

We glorify You, praise You and magnify Your name: protect our president from destruction and shame.

Shine Your light on the liars, the deceivers, the plotters: expose schemes and bring forth their names!

FEMALE DUMB DOWN

Men are tired being told there's something wrong with them.

Men are tired of being blamed for women's unhappiness.

Why aren't you married? Men: "Women aren't women anymore"

We finally have real men in charge(accusers) not a bunch of country club losers, boozers or cruisers.

I'm sorry but men aren't supposed to be women, or gay, or transgender--men should be real men!

Diseugenics: Each generation gets worse until it's hell on earth.

Have no illusions over liberals, they're gonna go their way. It's ideology not truth—what a tragic day.

False prophets introduce destructive heresies, denying the Lord and quickly self-destructing ~ 2 Peter 2:1

They disowned you first so now you disown them. They either give heart or give em heel, amen.

It is ridiculous for a woman of her caliber to dress like that. Nothing worse: an aging hippy and fat.

The wicked get caught in their own net. They made their bed by shooting at you, I'll bet.

Hankering for old systems putting you down is a sign you've lost God who makes you renowned.

All fear is based on focusing on the enemy rather than the assured victory, incredibly.

A conservative lady thinks ahead and plans her life accordingly. She never gives in to the disorderly:

Peak of sexual market value (SMV) is 20's but they are bedhopping not marriage shopping.

It happens: Women control in 20's but at 30 roles reverse as SMV--biological value to men--plummets.

The more she ages the harder it is to attract a high-value man.

The man's SMV increases after 30 with the acquiring of influence and resources.

That's why traditional women value a man's honesty, loyalty and hard work not his looks first.

How to be a success: de-confuse by not being so accessible, constantly reacting to the rabble.

Don't mal-adapt to insanity by becoming insane. Don't get dirty just cuz you live in the mud, ok?

Be audacious. The thing that got Janis Joplan was immorality bringing sudden ruin (hazardous).

Look how easily you falls in love--though many are frauds you fall again, "smitten" is a fool's chagrin.

Ditch the dumbed and gravitate to the smart. You do this and your life will catapult up, so start.

COMMIE NUTHOUSE

Capitalism relieves misery and brings people out of poverty--it's the single greatest thing for liberty. Trump is am exemplar: it's all about business, contracts and life as a war. But since the sixties communist thinking was forced on our country: law abiding folk loving freedom and liberty. The liberals are actually fascists and Trump's the only one not on the take--the rest are bought and sold, their rhetoric fake. Liberal contracts are situational ethics—not what is *right* but what they *want* {and how they taunt].

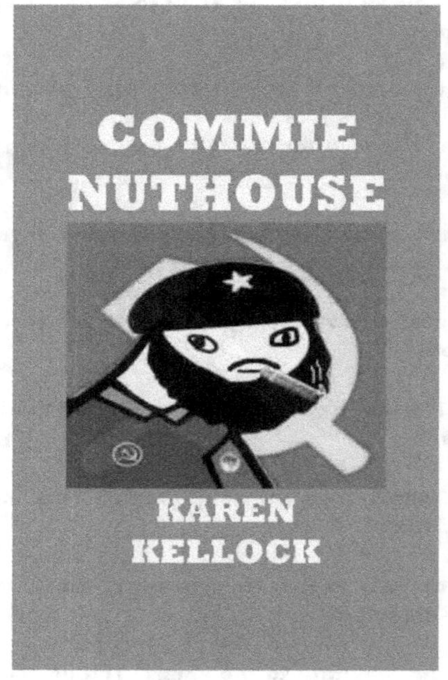

COMMIE NUTHOUSE

Or Luxurious Penthouse?

LIBERAL CONTRACTS ARE SITUATIONAL ETHICS
KKK: KRAZY KOLLEGE KIDS
MEN GIVEN A BAD RAP
CLINTON AND NAME RECOGNITION
FUTURE CAN BE BRIGHT—OR NOT
CONSTANT PROOF OF CRAZY YOUTH
EUPHEMISMS FOR PEDOPHILES
OBAMA FOMENTED RACE WARS
YOUR JOB: SHOW THE WORLD GOD
BLEND OF TRIVIAL AND IMPORTANT
PUPPETS ARE STILL TO BLAME
MOCKING SEX BECOMES A HEX
DEMOCRATS TO THE FAR LEFT
CORRUPT GOVERNMENT HATES TRUMP
NON-FACTS: COPS SHOOTING BLACKS
BEYONCE IS A TRAITOR TOO
LIBERALS LOVE TYRANNY
CORRUPTION: THE END OF THE HIPPY
HOLLYWOOD DICTATES CULTURE
THE WHOLE WORLD IS WAKING UP!
OBAMA A SLAVE TO DICTATORS
DISGUSTING, CRIMINAL, RUTHLESS WITCHES
THE WHITE MAN ENDED SLAVERY
LIBERALS WANNA KILL BABIES
THE PUBLIC BUYS INTO BULL
GANGS DISGUISED AS PEACE GROUPS
HISTORY SHOWS: EVIL IS WEAK

COMMIE NUTHOUSE
Or Luxurious Penthouse?

Sick witch feminists don't care one bit about the fate of women let alone men across the world.

Feminists in Cologne handing out roses to migrants just weeks after the rape-fest--what? Hello!

We know who they are. We wasted so much time with these liberal RINOS who think they're stars.

Since the sixties this crap was forced on our country: law abiding, decent folk loving freedom and liberty.

Trump's the only one not on the take. The rest are bought and sold--their rhetoric is fake.

Let Donald Trump be your absolute exemplar. It's all about business, contracts and life as a war.

LIBERAL CONTRACTS ARE SITUATIONAL ETHICS

Liberal contracts: it's all situational ethics--what *they* want. It changes too, as they taunt.

They act so silly and selfish, these so-called liberals. They're actually fascists though they seem so amiable.

Capitalism relieves misery and brings people out of poverty. It's the single greatest thing for liberty.

Trump picked up the delegates from candidates only getting 10%. When we won: what a thrilling event!

I've had it with Fox and won't give em another chance. It's more boring each time I give em a glance.

COMMIE NUTHOUSE

Having been brought up in government schools they think it's all theirs, so be armed and have spares.

When I finally saw how FOX sux I got my own life back and it totally rocks as I speak to the flock.

Ignore it all and just listen to Trump. That's how to spend your day--with music, nature and the sun.

The Krazy Kollege Kids just make me sick. After millions died for our freedom they put us up a creek.

Around bad leaders there is perversion. There is no decency with tyrants but with Trump it's revolution.

The kids are evil upstarts ruining our lives. We had it so good and fortunately Trump can now revive.

Of course they're evil--look at the things they accept! That's how you tell: from debates don't defect.

KKK: KRAZY KOLLEGE KIDS

The Krazy Kollege Kid Kulture is a bunch of lascivious liberals. They'll accept anything if it's social.

The whole feminist movement was absolutely horrible. It meant abortion and families were disabled.

Take a vacation as we let Trump take care of it all. This is a giant release as finally we can walk tall.

The new offense is "hurting someone's feelings". This is just a front for tyranny--the beginnings.

The left is the most killing organization in history. Break down the family, create hell and ruin society.

Goal: Total dictatorship with elites at the top exempt from all laws. It's college kids this draws!

COMMIE NUTHOUSE

Girl power: "We don't care if she kills, cheats, lies or steals--she's a woman": what a tragic omen.

We must educate our children locally—with love. Not federally with cold bureaucrats above.

Gun free zones are like candy for a baby. The sickos love em as we lose our liberty.

We're angry because we're run by incompetent people who are also immoral, filled with evil.

They use communist terms like "better world for all" or "create the future" which is bull by nature.

Our guy's getting so good I listen to him several times a day. All else pales cuz Trump's the Only Way.

MEN GIVEN A BAD RAP

Men have been given such a bad rap. It's disgusting how they're put down in this feminist/globalist fad.

When there's landslides they can't go against popular will. Stealing only works when close, as a rule.

Academia has gone far left and it's frightening. The left has taken over all education and it's disturbing.

Using the issue of race to advance their careers! That is horrible since it's creating race wars.

The more they control social institutions the easier it is to cause chaos which allows divide and rule.

When a leader's heart is right, you know he speaks the truth--it's Donald vs. the vile and uncouth!

Donald is the symbol of prospeprity and overnight success once rid of this mess.

COMMIE NUTHOUSE

We've won! Donald's a successful businessman, a giant success who knows how to get things done.

They escape judgment by denying Trump--though they voted for him in private, cowardly chumps.

Let the government get massive--that's more for us when we takeover. Spying too if we're clever.

CLINTON AND NAME RECOGNITION

Clinton. It's all about name recognition and identity politics: vote for Hillary because she's a woman.

Poets and cartoonists make their point fastest. That's why they're killed by dictators and fascists.

O. did it on purpose to show us who's who and flushed out foes as those who know came to blows.

When a doctor says "how's your sex life?" that isn't medicine, it's creepy feminism sneaking in.

Slick lies on FOX against Trump while force-feeding us Rubio--yuk! They're goin down: FOX SUX.

We're in the hands of such scum! But our military's in revolt at the highest levels so we'll be ok, hon.

The liberal gov is unelected and tyrannical, influencing police training manuals too ya know.

Their brainwashing is so complete they can't listen to reason. Just prepare, for this is your season.

The Art of the Deal man is the only one to untie the knot with these other deals we bought.

A terrible war begins and everything hangs in the balance. If leftist judge gets in: no liberty/no guns.

COMMIE NUTHOUSE

I will surely miss the supposed peace about this place. But I've looked at the wider issue: it's a police state.

Each state is different in cultural psychology--since it's the leadership which determines policy.

Where we're going the conservative's kids are so nice compared to these who couldn't care less.

So when choosing a new state, look at the politics--guns, regulations, human rights, taxes--good luck.

The tiny California town I lived in seems peaceful. But that's almost an omen of the future upheaval.

If your state's led by a tax-and-spend "progressive" then you'll have police state problems--just sayin'.

FUTURE CAN BE BRIGHT—OR NOT

The future of our country is bright! It's all because so many are waking up to reality, overnight!

Those of us who study things closely see a pattern that makes us certain its curtains.

We see patterns, we get gut feelings then we see proof indicators. That's not a talent in your deniers.

It is hard to leave California as I'm addicted to the beauty and dry heat but it's filled with liberal deceit.

We have the right and duty to demand the removal of any tyrannical government, amen.

He's aiding and abetting the enemy, a most serious charge against the people now seeking remedy.

It takes divine intervention or catastrophe to wake Americans up. Pray the divine comes through Trump.

COMMIE NUTHOUSE

Kanye and JZ types are constantly stirring stuff up to sell tickets: It's a sickness with the wicked.

Patriots fought to death defending the great experiment: America. Now it happebed again with Obama.

He wants to help us darn it, so get on the Trump bandwagon and don't listen to silly pundits!

Whenever in a muddle, ask "What would Trump do?" and that'll end the struggle with your troubles.

We're really mad after feeling bad but fortunately God raised a solution King and he's like our dad.

They fight for the slaughter of unborn children, they fight for perversion. We're at the cliff of destruction.

CONSTANT PROOF OF CRAZY YOUTH

The youth have gone crazy--this is proof. They also wanted Sanders, a socialist and goof.

Incredibly, I'm starting to appreciate CNN more than the fakes at Fox which sux (but used to rock).

Isn't America busted out with this? We're a laughing stock of the whole world with breast jobs gone amiss.

Like Donald says: "there's so little common sense!" Inverted from reality, we learned to be dense.

Their evil house of cards is falling so fast! That's how it always happens once people awake/become aghast.

Boys and girls aren't taught traditional gender roles any more so balanced households become disorder.

Drop TV/Fox and all arrogant scum. You've got a great job to do, untainted by the dumb.

COMMIE NUTHOUSE

Terrorism always exposes enablers in their flaccid response to evil. Greg Gutfeld

Trump's a Nietzschen figure: if you don't take him out he just gets stronger.

When they celebrate Trump losing, it's America's loss their applauding because they want that badly.

Dictating peace through strength: no one else can do it but we can by making America great again.

The liberal agenda: Safe space Orwellian social justice warrior new world order hell in America.

In the sixties hippies were called "loving" but now they're in power and it's tyranny (crushing).

It's a liberal worldview seeing all humans as deserving of rights even the most perverse: yikes!

EUPHEMISMS FOR PEDOPHILES

MAPS: Minor Attracted Persons (pedophiles)

Banned from twitter for right-wing views yet they're allowed to advocate pedophilia in youtube videos.

Pedophiles: Atheists disbelieving in good vs. evil so liberals never see them as truly bad people.

Anyone buying the leftist line--even one little slogan--will be less than he is and not well-spoken.

The Age of Cowardice is coming to an end just as the Age of Men is beginning to return, amen.

Tyrants say anyone trying to promote liberty is a "terrorist" and it's this us patriots must resist.

When liberals hear "Nazi" they think "right wing". But Hitler was a liberal socialist vegan who didn't drink.

COMMIE NUTHOUSE

Through Donald we can return from the brink. If you can't see the state we're in you need a shrink.

The message was: "don't mess with us". This was very serious as we faced terrible tyranny in the U.S.

The liberal publisher said "If we took out all the offensive parts there wouldn't be a book left"--complement.

The world's been waiting for a leader who speaks from the heart not phony teleprompters, for a start.

Dumb females love to rely on government. It's like their daddy since they've degraded real men.

Instead of modest sweet little ladies, women have become monsters listening to feminists so shady.

OBAMA FOMENTED RACE WARS

He was fomenting race wars, can't you see that? A true leader is a unifier not a dirty divisive rat.

"Trumpism": Expression of legitimate anger over American events and the belief only Trump can solve it.

Liberals have nothing to say, they're empty. It's all talking points, party lines and whatever's trendy.

The 5-4 SCOTUS majority was the only check on the left's gov expansion to take all of our property.

From London to New York people's heads are down, terrified. That's what happens with lost pride.

America: This leader has beat us up daily and many feel chagrin. You must feel big and proud again.

Revitalization Movements led by one with charisma bring sudden reversals-- prosperity in America!

COMMIE NUTHOUSE

God help us, the country's been betrayed! But we can still come back if enough of us prayed.

Adapting to liberal culture brings grossness. A grossification of America has occurred, replacing greatness.

They get upset all day about things that don't matter. That's the left and feminists lost in chatter.

It's never been so urgent for men to find their male side (the animus) by rising up (despite feminists).

People are waking up in huge numbers! Thank you God for opening minds previously encumbered.

YOUR JOB: SHOW THE WORLD GOD

Your job is to show the world God--how He's way higher than the mob of liberals and other slobs.

For decades leftism has meant destruction under the veil of "loving tolerance" but it is the devil.

God raises up leaders at the perfect time. They're perfect for the job and defy the party line.

All through history are revitalization movements. Always led by a charismatic One—this is it.

The man: The One who can bring it all together, from coal mining to feminist wives under the weather.

If you're against guns (the great equalizer) you're not a feminist and want women to be defenseless.

Just for speaking truth they'll call you "mean"--having adapted to the smiling phony fiends.

We're winning the information war: People waking up to this crap so fast and it's opening all doors!

COMMIE NUTHOUSE

FOX News is as bad as the rest--stealing the narrative and throwing it in your face--but it's collapsing, alas.

FOX is just Collaborators Stealing the Narrative, so ban it while seeing the falsehood of it.

This is how the news lies: not just by omission but framing things in certain ways--days in a daze.

History is being made. The media establishment is collapsing before our eyes and it's clear they lied.

Ignore 99% of what you hear. This gives you much found time--it's exhilarating, dear.

Don't be weak in front of other men, they may drug you. That's help-seeking in the wrong avenues.

BLEND OF TRIVIAL AND IMPORTANT

Just the proportion of trivial vs. important news is a way of lying: It's how you frame it darlin'

Now is the time for all good men to come forward to the center: We're calling out all inventors!

Realize how different you are having standards, ethics and morals--and be alert/ready for scoundrels.

Confirmed: Rubio was in bed with Murdoch at Fox. I tell you this backdoor manipulation just sux.

Banned means banned. When someone shows their obvious bias you must reject and nothing less.

In joking against Trump, Cruz made a complete fool of himself and fell like a rock. Genius is: Trump.

After eight years of extreme anguish we deserve a vacation. Work for Trump with community organizin'.

COMMIE NUTHOUSE

Eight years we've endured extreme anguish as we saw our country dismantled and bashed.

Trust very few and decide who they are. Stop getting hurt by tolerance now proven wrong by far.

He wanted to kill us in the time he had left. Here are the consequences to elections: poverty and death.

Trump's an exemplar for the rest of us--of not taking any more crap after losing all our trust.

Many candidates are "limp handshakes" compared to our man Trump. Sense this then dump.

PUPPETS ARE STILL TO BLAME

Though a puppet he's still to blame--selling our soul to the devil as millions see their lives leveled.

I didn't feel in the clear, he could do so much damage in under a year and we had plenty to fear.

The Lord has spoke! We'll get behind Trump and pray it's not a yoke but he'll make us rich not broke.

Every so often a Great Leader is risen up by God, His answer to devastating circumstances and fraud.

God raises a genius to meet the need! That's due to His magnificent mercy: answering with speed.

Hillary and all the RINOS have tanked. It'd be good if they'd now go Trump for the highest rank.

All FOX talks about is her emails all day, never pointing out her huge crimes which they hide away.

If Hillary gets in she's gonna move against the people and we'll be in so much trouble: evil.

COMMIE NUTHOUSE

We can't stand to see his evil face. His name is Destruction and we hate this liar, fraud and disgrace.

Mentally ill women into power-tripping with cult leader mommy Hillary: I have them in my own family.

It is not our government--just a bunch of cronies screwing us over and they're all phonies.

Hillary/RINOS tanked when fraud stepped in (that's always how they do it) but Trump's a shoe in.

Dam dems please leave cuz (you're for evil things and) you always have fraud up your sleeve.

Trump wants to be Geo Washington so let him! He's the only one not-bought and history will love him.

MOCKING SEX BECOMES A HEX

The New Age, medicine and feminism make a mockery of sex with prying questions--it's a hex.

Sex is sacred but the glib and casual way they talk about it is so embarrassing--shut up!

Yes, Bush was terrible but nothing compared to Obama. America's in ruins, we all feel trauma.

Doctors: "Bleeding, difficulty breathing, trouble seeing--and BTW, How's your sex life?" (I'm unbelieving).

They don't come and take the guns, they infringe it on the edges--gradually we see the changes.

The founders said the feds are not superior to the states and the individual is sovereign--same weights.

The officious lascivious questions of doctors do embarrass, are needless and come from feminists.

COMMIE NUTHOUSE

We must eliminate the excessive use of force--whether we agree with victims or not, of course.

Trump is Scotch: Our brave heart is about freedom and shrewd business deals in God's kingdom.

Fox repeated "Marco Rubio's on a Surge..." Not true, it was Trump they sought to submerge.

They make out like bandits and the worst part is we've allowed it by our nonchalance, so stop it!

They're crude, lewd with big fake boobs. That's new age taught in the schools by feminist fools.

Don't tell me Christ never got angry--he tipped over tables! We're told to hate evil and all else is fables.

The Nazis used mosquitos as bio-weapons to poison the foe. Bill Gates does this now you know.

FOX sux: "Cruz is surging and Trump is failing". It was just the opposite from what they were saying.

DEMOCRATS TO THE FAR LEFT

The democrats have moved so far to the left, away from basic American values and vital issues.

The democrats are well-versed in dirty tricks: cutting corners, killing foes and calling patriots hicks.

Mad how I've wasted years on FOX--a total waste of time but it takes what it takes to see what sux.

The democrats protect devils. They are anathema both here and Europe--a stench in God's nostrils.

Liberals work to protect criminals who've robbed and murdered, yet kill babies--doesn't that make you ill?

COMMIE NUTHOUSE

Constrain TV choices to Classic Movies and the History Channel. All else is waste--leftist and modern.

The great thing about being black is no one can call you a racist for putting down this present fascist.

Highly motivated people who love liberty--these are the Christians who desperately want stability.

Corrupt government does not want things changed so they hate Trump and want Hillary (deranged).

CORRUPT GOVERNMENT HATES TRUMP

Corrupt government hates Trump cuz he's the only one coming against them/don't reject him.

Everybody but us—we the people--hates Trump cuz he can't be controlled by their evil.

Trump is the only one who can beat the system cuz he doesn't need what the system uses, amen.

Even as the media trashes Trump he surged and prevailed but they pumped the others up meanwhile.

Since when does the sanctity of life mean a war against women's health? Since libs said it: filth.

The liberal "climate change style" of broad, indistinct and meaningless generalizations is boring.

They say to media heads: "Either do what we say on Trump or we yank your advertisers", yes sir.

They're giving millions of dollars to stop Trump. The media must do this or risk being dumped.

The power Trump has is at the top, the liberal misperceptions at the bottom (which never stops).

COMMIE NUTHOUSE

This is our country we're losing. Not a football game but the real deal--forever, if they win.

I turned on FOX to see what's happening. It was so boring, so nothing, such silly laughing...

It's not about outright lying but obfuscation and no transparency. For bad tactics have no leniency.

They plant audiences, then by their reactions try to shift opinions--by booing Trump's words and visions.

They're lulled into complacency by milquetoast media and all their friends think the same: seedy.

If their reactions to what you say are liberal, don't give em a thought cuz they're really horrible.

You know that patriot who was shot dead by the feds? He was my neighbor in Cane Beds.

NON-FACTS: COPS SHOOTING BLACKS

Police targeting of black people is a blatant lie disproven many times but Beyonce uses it as lines.

Turned Fox on, just to "see". It was boring and chillingly empty--withdrawal from addiction makes us free!

Rainbow, Black Panther: Halftime celebration of democrat social platform as if LBGT is the norm!

Democrat social issues: Teaching filth to our kids. How did this perversion ever happen—be rid!

Filth taught to our kids is called "values clarification"--but we never agreed to this degradation!

Imagine teaching pornography to five year olds! That's how Common Core ruins our households.

COMMIE NUTHOUSE

What made America great was our moral foundation. We need to revert back: Revolution!

'I've unliked your pages, deleted your songs and will never buy a thing from either of you."--ex-Biance fan.

How did we allow this filth to take over? We've reached our breaking point--it's about our future!

Breaking point: Separate from bad associations going along with this filth for they ruined our spirit.

The Super Bowl: when Americans unite to watch our game 'til Beyonce divided us (bad dame).

FOX was my addiction (I needed it more but enjoyed it less) since I'm a scholar but it was fiction.

BEYONCE IS A TRAITOR TOO

Beyonce is as much a traitor as Jane Fonda was in the sixties. Dividing us is causing violence swiftly!

We now have hope. What a relief after eight years of pure hell, every day feeling unequally yoked.

The college students are sickeningly stupid, having been deliberately dumbed and brainwashed (twisted).

The most twisted are called "intellectuals". They make stuff up and we're forced to accept it all.

Trump wants to give back to a country that has given him so much. He will fix things with a magic touch!

Gloria Steinem says feminists stand against Islam sexism? What a joke, they do not, Ms. Steinem!

The left's lawlessness has awoken the sleeping giant of Christians demanding prosperity and freedom.

COMMIE NUTHOUSE

Rubio tast-tracked the TPP! What a terrible turncoat, and Fox wants this candidate, see?

Rubio is the front man for the Open Borders Syndicate. He's like a third term for Obama, let's face it.

Gun background checks will lead to confiscation which will lead to tyrannical government.

Trump is the only light in the darkness of theft, murder and debauchery. He is the only one, surely.

Arrogance is blindness and deviants are devious. That's why we hate these things: they're insidious.

The progressive left stands down with Islamists. Incredibly, this alliance also includes the feminists.

LIBERALS LOVE TYRANNY

The soft liberals love tyranny and re-education camps cuz they haven't experienced the dumps.

You reap what you sow. You've left death/destruction from Libya to Russia-- death to your soul.

Conservatives give more to charity than wealthy liberals. The "loving" leftists are often criminals.

Liberals are six times more likely to steal while claiming they give to charity (but not = bad deals).

Gloria Steinem is an enemy of women and humanity. She won't expose FGM and Sharia law tragedies.

Hillary hired people to intimidate her husband's rape victims. And this you call feminist wisdom?

The west is the best place for women yet the feminists put it down constantly: I detest!

COMMIE NUTHOUSE

Hell is a place where there is no reason. Anonymous

The left started arrogant but in jeans. Now they're in fashion suits lording it over us like fiends.

"Sustainable" is all about controlling people--not making things better just dragging it to the gutter.

Trump will defeat the enemies. A change in the minds/hearts of many will grow into a Tsunami.

Delusions of left for show: Those who know will always know, those who don't, never (the foe).

CORRUPTION: THE END OF THE HIPPY

Corruption is: committing murders and taking money, mostly--and thus ends the era of the hippy.

Two groups in America: the ruling class and everyone it favors, then everyone else. Donald Trump

Thanks alot you Krazy Kollege Kids and BLM. Cops won't answer calls and we're going into mayhem.

Art is no longer about creating and transcending but virtue signaling and justice warrior leading.

Foment a riot then go out as the peace maker. We don't buy it anymore from this leftist faker.

We were color blind when we voted for him but now we're over it yet he wasn't, to our chagrin.

It is racism, you're right! ! I am not safe due to the color of my skin, which is white.

Recall Soul Train, how they could dance and dress? We admired them much but that's racist I guess.

COMMIE NUTHOUSE

Liberals are forever finding phony moral equivalence between disparate things--how sickening.

God wants our freedom. Knowing that, we feel upheld by the Master of the universe, amen.

Trump's a Presbyterian, which means he is Calvinist: He believes in his destiny to be the best.

Most Trump hatred comes from jealousy. You can see it in many men who hate with a fury.

HOLLYWOOD DICTATES CULTURE

Hollywood dictates culture, pushing a liberal agenda. First it's about this, then that, now gender.

You can always count on Americans to do the right thing--after trying everything else. Winston Churchill

Social justice warriors are stupified through schools via slogans: Consciences seared, spirits broken.

The self-inflicted curse is called "political correctness" but I tell you truthfully, it is mental illness.

If they insist 2 + 2 = 5, and hold to that with vitriol, then you give up on them totally, that's all.

They have to get mad because their silly arguments collapse when faced with reason: how sad.

It's phony, fake, fraudulent and sleazy--so don't go along with any part of it and stay busy.

You see it on the surface and look deeper--it just gets worse. That's the way of sinners, then the hearse.

They're corrupt, fallen and playing with fire. They thus bring themselves down, the liars.

COMMIE NUTHOUSE

Psychopaths building an artificial reality ready to insert us into it and we're buying it, really.

"White privilege" is just a way to bludgeon you and tell you to shut up, born with a bad rep.

It is racist to assume that white people have privilege over everyone else but that's the whole fuss.

"Anti-free speech goons" have taken over. They know nothing, use tantrums for this hostile takeover.

Social justice warriors: mentally stunted toddlers who throw fits, scream and refuse to follow orders.

The Christian seeks to keep couples together while the secular seeks to keep them apart.

THE WHOLE WORLD IS WAKING UP!

The whole world's waking up and they love Trump! It's a world revolution: fill thy cup!

Cycles: It's when things get worse that revival comes. There is great suffering, then the fun.

My uncle age 102 said cycles get so bad then swing back to normalcy--I pray it's true what he said.

God sees the truth but waits. The patriots see the amoral traitor but also know his fate.

It all comes together in a personality toppling the old regime, settling doubts about fiends.

To make clear the words of the tribe: That's our job as artists on cultural treachery we describe.

A nation can survive fools and the ambitious, but it cannot survive treason from within. Cicero

COMMIE NUTHOUSE

He appeals to baseness lying deep in the hearts of all men while he rots the soul of a nation.

He lied about history and created a false moral equivalency between us and them (ugly and gory).

The gov. should not pick winners and losers but lift obstacles to innovation like SWAT abusers.

The America I love accounted for 90% of the world's greatest inventions, so shut up man.

It's "in" to hate Trump but you gotta think for yourself, stupid. See right and the bands of evil loosens.

Christians were tormented in their secular families: Made to feel like small and stupid anomalies.

The number one shamer of decent Americans was in the whitehouse and he was a fake and a louse.

OBAMA A SLAVE TO DICTATORS

He was a slave to dictators and a dictator to his own people and believe me it was total evil.

Distorted, twisted worldviews: that's the common trendy in the West, spoiled rotten too.

There is not one but two paths: one narrow to God and one wide conforming to the mob.

Anti-intellectual elitism dismisses science and history, replaced by self-righteous ignorance and gullibility.

I never thought I'd live in a time where my own president would bring down his own country.

Watch how enlightenment is a chain reaction. All they need is someone reaching out to them.

COMMIE NUTHOUSE

They took over but now that the hoax is gone--it's game over! We've won, the freedom-lovers.

Our time has come: No longer called dumb by liberals (until we became it from being numb).

Nothing feels so good as inversion of systems as the bottom becomes the top and they're all flops!

Enontiodromia: A life phase when everything reverses as we rise up and God fills our purses!

Liberals had it out for conservative Christians and it got dirty. But now it's reversing, surely.

To think how we had to adapt to their filthiness. Though we're all sinners, at least we rejected this.

DISGUSTING, CRIMINAL, RUTHLESS WITCHES

Disgusting, criminal, ruthless, heartless Hillary witch--and your sister voted for this bitch?

We've already won just by getting Trump in. Just by bringing out the truth, God's in agreement.

The truth can no longer be suppressed! It's out and we're gonna win (no more depressed)!

It's a war between those who want the new world order vs. the constitution and the founders!

Christians who mal-adapted to liberal logic by lives tragic will now have a rebound: fantastic!

You will now see God's vengeance on those who held you down while you become renowned!

It was simply tragic how God-lovers adapted to liberal logic for 40 years but now life is magic!

COMMIE NUTHOUSE

Many had liberals in their families--serial bullies! They ruined our lives but now it's all goodies.

Now the Superior Man comes from the periphery to the center, cuz he repented after being a sinner.

They got off on lying to their audience as we confused his spiffy looks/glibness for "goodness".

Nowhere in history has there been a leader where everything is a lie causing so much misery.

THE WHITE MAN ENDED SLAVERY

The white man didn't start slavery, he ended it. He didn't usurp discovery, he invented it.

There's a chance we won't go into destruction as Trump will save us instead, no need to dread.

There's a consequence to liberal governance in your city and it is horrible (not pretty).

Liberals are beta male wanna-be elitists who are against our guns so they may defeat us.

Only beta males act dominant--true alphas are seething with energy and more confident.

The Bible, US constitution and Bill of Rights: our common cultural heritage is worthy of the fight.

All TV even Fox dump on Trump 24 hours a day so the public is turned off, going away.

Once a culture goes under centralized control it always collapses but liberals want our ashes.

Whenever you hear words like "sustainable" or Yale, think liberal. The brightest are fools.

COMMIE NUTHOUSE

There are fools in Washington but also traitors. Power brings out the evil inner nature.

Liberals want to kill innocent babies in the womb but keep murderers alive-- that's true, no jive.

What passes for IQ is social hypnotism. The herd thinks it's truth only because it's in.

Liberals want babies killed not hardened criminals and I've had enough of these fools.

Christians can mal-adapt to liberals by getting sicker than them, who control like scum.

The bathroom thing is a fork in the road--the litmus test of sanity and who's a prince or a toad.

LIBERALS WANNA KILL BABIES

Liberals wanna kill babies and let criminals go free. This is the type of those hating liberty.

Christians get much sicker adapting to liberals than the controllers themselves--ouch!

Based on a false premise: liberals proliferate rules, regulations and perverse relations.

Liberals wanna kill babies and let criminals go free and these haters of liberty stink to me.

There IS a cultural psychology to regions and states. Utah is great California I hate.

My mind snapped when Obama got in. Now with the prospect of Trump, I am well again!

Cultural Marxism is involved with sexual perversion. Think of the sixties hippies (and education).

COMMIE NUTHOUSE

Arrest development in the population and you can induce mass mental illness in them.

When Christians adapt to liberals they get much sicker then the latter takes control--the kicker.

The minute I entered school I felt out of place and panic-stricken as my soul was sickened.

Liberals are arrogant creeps. That's the truth peeps so now clear em out: clean sweep.

Stripped of true rights we're given faux rights: to go to the wrong bathroom with out a fight.

God uses the ungodly to accomplish his plans when the godly can't fill the bill nor understand.

Only six percent trust in the mainstream media--it is only evil and devious tedium.

They play it up! It's show business for ugly people. Lame-stream news are liars and evil.

THE PUBLIC BUYS INTO BULL

As the public buys into the bull there's more delusion, mental illness and numbskulls.

They wanna be on a hill with helicopters while we're down here in shacks paying a high tax.

It's not a "conspiracy theory" but in front of us, happening--while liberals stay blind, napping.

You have so much to be proud of in yourself. You're not a liberal and love God and the True Self.

Trumpists are the smartest and most highly educated people but libs call them dumb and evil.

COMMIE NUTHOUSE

So what if he's repetitive--some things demand underscoring and his imploring is never boring.

Nazis were radical homosexual socialists and now they're the bathroom rights antagonists.

Love of little babies the liberals call "fetal idolatry" cuz they're so cold-blooded about their atrocity.

I used to think if we put women in power everything would be better but I grew beyond this fetter.

Some religions equate being very social with godliness. Thus the introvert is evil, I guess.

Many confuse being "social" with being Christian. Learn to say "NO" and get something done.

GANGS DISGUISED AS PEACE GROUPS

It's gangs disguised as "peace groups". That's the leftist vermin to whom you must not stoop.

Have you seen the racism of a black guy punching an innocent white man in the head, dead?

Obama released the tattooed gang bangers just in time for the election--and no objection.

Krazy Kollege Kids have gotten away with blocking speech for so long: entitled and headstrong.

Beck calls Trumpians "morons and uneducated hicks". It's really the opposite, but that's politics.

There's a psychology to regions and states. Where I live now: liberty, California: tyranny

It's way better getting out of liberalville California. Though it's going pro-Trump, it's about the liberal aura.

They've all gone along with the crap and perversions he has propounded as president.

They're teaching "fake rebellion". Stirring things up so they really feel like truly abused victims.

Victory arrives from (1) confidence and (2) historical understanding of how the enemy operates.

There's an attack on the species by a guild of psychopaths that must be defeated—believe it.

I have the inside on PETA and it's not what you think of it. Actually it is opposite, not legit.

They intend to take over entirely, but all they do is sow the seeds of their own destruction, mightily.

HISTORY SHOWS: EVIL IS WEAK

History shows: evil is weak, but wins by convincing people they have no power/are up a creek.

We want property rights and our freedoms for everyone not this fake crap like victimization.

Let's toast to the collapsing phony leftist media! Finally arrogance shuts those up loving Obama.

Keep the momentum going (we're not snatched from the jaws of hell yet) but awareness is showing.

Liberals--fake pseudo-intellectuals--aren't laughing now! Soon we're rid of those who love Mao.

He senses destiny and loves America and prosperity. It's victory and we're celebrating today.

This is a victory for the people! A Revitalization Movement and Donald Trump is only the symbol.

COMMIE NUTHOUSE

The traitors wanna tax us for the air we breathe. So of course it's Trump in whom we believe.

We've been held back (censured) by liberals for forty years! This is explosive after many tears.

Arrogant liberals said "We are sovereigns--you don't get to vote" as leftist insanity spoke.

"We are royalty" the arrogant creeps said. Jewels in pig snouts describe the leftist scumbags.

100 KAREN KELLOCK BOOKS

AFFINITY OR MISERY
AGELESS CORNUCOPIA
AMERICA AWAKE!
AMERICA'S DAFT ERA
ARTS OF PALEO FASTING
AUTOPHAGY ON CHEATERS
BACKSTABBING NEUROTICS
BETRAYAL TRAUMA
BOOMERS AND BROKENNESS
BOOT ON NECK
CHAMPION GUIDES
COMMIE NUTHOUSE
COMMIES
COMMUNIST SPIRIT
CONTAGION OF MADNESS
CONTAGIOUS MADNESS
CULTURE CLASH BASHED
DAFT LEFT
DAILY FASTARIAN
DAM RATS
DIVERSITY IS CRUELTY
E-RACE WHITE
EVIL FREAKS (Beyond Gross)
THE END OR A BEND?
FEMALE BULLIES AND FEMI-NAZIS
FEMALE CARNALITY
FEMALE DUMB DOWN
FEMALE POWER DRIVE
FEMINISM AND RUIN 1 & 2
FIX FOR MISFITS
FOOLS & TRAMPS
FREEDOM SPEAKING
FRENEMY ENABLER
FRENEMY LIAR
FRENEMY THIEF
FRENEMY TRAITOR
TRENEMY TYRANT
GENIUS IS HELD DOWN
GLOBALISLAM
GOD USES THE FLAWED
HAZE OF THE LATTER DAYS

THE HERD IN WORDS
HIX POLITIX
HOW THEY RUINED US
JUST SKIP DINNER
LE FEMME AND THE COMMUNIST SPIRIT
LIBERAL CHAOS & ROT
LIBERAL DOUBLETHINK
LIBERAL GALL 1 & 2
LIBERAL SHOVE-DOWNS
LOCK YOUR GATE
LOSERS and Femme Fatales
MANUAL FOR SUPERIOR MEN
MODERN ART FROM HELL
MOSTLY FAKE
NOTES TO CHAMPS 1 & 2
OVERCOME FRENEMIES
PC MAKES US CRAZY
PEOPLE ARE CRUEL
PEOPLE PROBLEMS 1 & 2
PERSECUTED GENIUIS
POLI-PSYCH MYSTERIES
PRETENTIOUS SLOBS
QUEEN BEE
RED NEW DEAL
RETURNING TO FIRST NATURE
SEASON OF TREASON
SEPARATE MEANS HOLY
SOCIAL HYPNOTISM
SOLITUDE SOLUTION
SUPERCILIOUS
THE SCHOOLS SCREWED EM UP
TOAD TO PRINCE
TRIALS CYCLES
TRUMP VS. GROUP
TRUST IN TRASH
THE TRUTH ABOUT PEOPLE
UNDERHEANDEDLY CLEVER
WALK TALL WITHIN WALLS
WE'RE NOT ALL ONE
WINNERS SKIP DINNER
WORK OR SMERK

KAREN KELLOCK PH.D.

M.S. Political Science, San Diego State. Ph.D. in Psychology, University of California Irvine. Postdoctoral: UCI School of Medicine, Dept. of Psychiatry [NIMH Grants]. Developed the Debris Theory of Disease, a theory of system pathology in 120 books and 22 textbooks for the general public. The theory has a general formula: All disease is obstruction, all recovery is elimination, all success is attraction. The three obstructions are people, habit and food. Remove obstruction and snap to your goals, waiting in the wings.